Before reading this book, the r

- two or more letters can represe
- the spellings ‹air› ‹are› ‹ere› can represent ...

This book introduces:
- the spellings ‹air› ‹are› ‹ere› for the sound 'air'
- text at 2 syllable level

High-frequency words:
tooth, into, room, she, said, her, 50p, for, foot, now, I, didn't, was, would, see, out, of, under, so, don't, be, my, you

Vocabulary:
declared – said something clearly and openly
careless – not taking care or clumsy
despair – a feeling of no hope

Talk about the story

When Fred loses his tooth, Clair, the fairy, comes to give him 50p. But Clair is careless and drops the 50p. How will she find it in the dark? Will Fred wake up?

Reading Practice

Practise blending these sounds into words:

air	are	ere
fair	care	there
pair	hare	where
hair	dare	
chair	fare	
stairs	glare	
unfair	rare	
haircut	share	

Careless Fairy

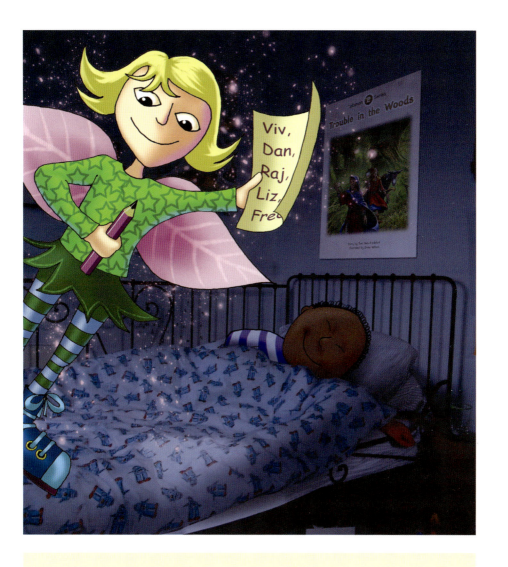

When Fred lost his tooth, Clair, the fairy, whizzed into his room.

"There is Fred!" she said.

Clair dug in her bag. "50p for Fred's tooth!" she declared.

Then she dropped the 50p.

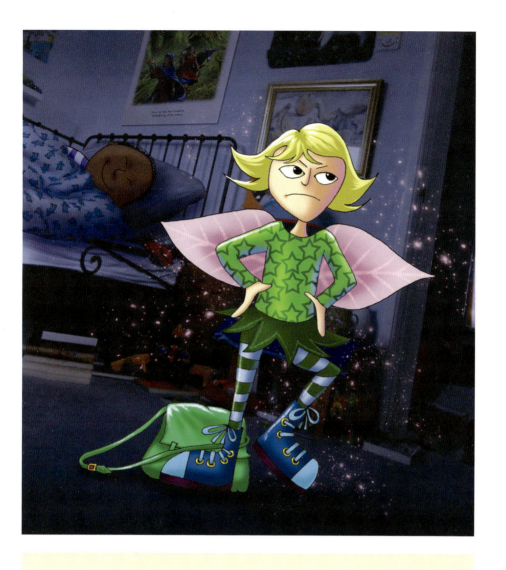

Clair stamped her foot. "Now where is that 50p? I am such a careless fairy!" she said.

Clair didn't dare switch on the light. She was scared that Fred would see her. "Where is that 50p?"

"There it is!" Fred jumped out of bed and got it from under the chair. Clair stared at him.

"I am so careless!" said Clair in despair. "Don't be sad," said Fred, "I will share my cards with you."

Questions for discussion:

- Why does Clair, the fairy, have a list of names?

- Why did Clair bring Fred a 50p coin?

- Why does Clair say she is a 'careless fairy'?

Game with ‹air›, ‹are› and ‹ere› words

Play as pelmanism or use for reading practice. Enlarge and photocopy the page twice on two different colours of card. Cut the cards up to play.
Ensure the players sound out the words.

fair	care	rare
glare	there	stairs
unfair	hare	air
share	where	haircut